Dedicated to creative mamas everywhere

CONTENTS

2. HOW TO USE THIS WORKBOOK

4. INTRODUCTION - VALIDATION

9. DISCLAIMER - DEDICATION

13. PART ONE: *INWARD*

    14) EXPECTATION

    20) INTUITION

    26) RECLAMATION

    32) RECOGNITION

39. INTERMISSION

    40) AFFIRMATION

44. PART TWO: *OUTWARD*

    45) PREPARATION

    48) COLLABORATION

    52) ACTIVATION

56. RESOURCES

58. GRATITUDE

59. CREDITS

60. MORE OFFERINGS FROM WHO'S YOUR MAMA

62–65. EXTRA JOURNALING SPACE

HOW TO USE THIS WORKBOOK

The flow of *The (Re)Discovering Creativity After Motherhood Workbook* is based on the stages of my own personal journey of (re)discovery (a journey I'm still on, by the way) so I highly suggest reading/working in chapter order. With that being said, **Part 1** is structured for mamas (re)discovering themselves from square one—exploring what sort of creativity/outlet they want to pursue in the first place; while **Part 2** is all action and forward motion and no looking back—the nitty-gritty *how* to the introspective *what*. Either way, be sure to start with my **Introduction** on the following pages. One of the most important first steps in *my* journey was the realization that *I was not alone* in how I was feeling ... so if validation and solidarity is what you're looking for, I'm your girl.

Looking for alternative ways to (Re)Discover?

To best allow mamas to (Re)Discover Creativity with intention, I chose to offer this workbook in "good ol' fashioned" printed paper format. However, for those who feel most comfortable behind a keyboard, I also created a (re)fillable **digital PDF version**, and **Video Lessons**, available for purchase online at <u>WhosYourMamaMedia.com</u>. I also offer local workshops for even more validation and accountability, in a welcoming group setting. Turn to the **More Offerings** section, or visit my website, to learn more.

Spread the word!

The offerings of **Who's Your Mama Media** are projects dear to my heart, and were created as my soul offering to the world. These are resources that I wish *I* had access to in those early days, and the more mamas I can support through these offerings, the better for them *(and for everyone)*. *So please, help spread the word to the mamas in your life by encouraging them to snag their own copy of this Workbook—and to check out all that Who's Your Mama has to offer—we all get by with a little help from our family and friends!*

"This is a conversation that moms need to have with each other. Just being real about how exhausted we are, because we are trying to be perfect moms, business owners, wives, friends ... the list just goes on."

- Kelly Covert,
inner voice coach & host of the *In Her Voice* podcast
(*Who's Your Mama* · Season 1 · Episode 19)

INTRODUCTION - VALIDATION

Yesterday I had a bit of a mama meltdown. You know the scene—Mama plans a culturally-enriching and enjoyable day out with child (multiplied by the number of children your reality includes). Child rushes through anything resembling fun, only to loudly complain that nothing is fun. Child refuses to eat pizza, because how dare mama torture him with the offer of pizza. Once home, child uses nap time not to sleep, but to loudly wail-sing the alphabet song on repeat two inches from the monitor and then poop all over the sheets mama just washed hours earlier, despite available potty next to toddler bed. Mama locks herself in bathroom to ugly-cry while texting husband/partner/mother/best friend/stranger: "I AM DONE WITH THIS CHILD." Not-napping, possibly naked, child gets unceremoniously bestowed on the first able-bodied human who walks in the door while crazy-eyed mama demands a single hour of alone-time to angrily "relax" while she practices some tainted semblance of #selfcare. *Too little, too late.*

And why does it have to reach that point? Why does shit figuratively (and sometimes literally) have to hit the fan before another adult offers to take over, or in an even less common scenario, mama actually asks for the help she so desperately needs? The familiar adage "it takes a village" isn't just some old wives' tale—it comes directly from a time (not too long ago, in fact) when helping hands were only a quick call, short walk, or single room away. It was family, friends, and neighbors. No judgment. Everyone was friendly and wanted to help. And receiving this help was easy, it was acceptable, and most importantly, it was simply how things were done.

When I first became a mother in the autumn of 2013, I didn't know about the importance of self-care. I didn't even know how to change a diaper, bless my heart. I didn't necessarily think motherhood was going to be all sunshine and unicorns, but I did think it was something I would just *know* how to do, like giving birth. And I didn't have many people in my life telling me otherwise. Don't get me wrong, I am forever thankful to those who told me "you look *FANTASTIC"* throughout every stage of my pregnancy (the only thing you should ever say to a pregnant woman, by the way), but I am especially in debt to those few, brave souls who gave it to me straight. Who told me There Will Be Blood during, and after, the birth. Who ignored the cute, but completely unnecessary, things on my registry and instead brought me a basket full of nipple cream, disposable breast pads and witch hazel. Who visited in those first days at home, not just to hold the baby, but to clean my house and make me spinach salad. Who were/are farther along this path than me and make sure I always know the truth about what's ahead, or that the truth happening to me now is not only normal, but happened to them as well.

Unfortunately, these few bright stars were hard to see in the early days—*the dark days*. Perhaps it was the especially harsh winter trapping us inside, or maybe I had the "baby blues." Quite possibly I had some level of post-partum depression (PPD) or anxiety (PPA)—undiagnosed because, again, *I didn't know!* What I did know was that I was completely overwhelmed, resentful, and operating under the (mistaken) impression—thanks to smiley advertising—that no one in the history of time had ever felt the way I was feeling. I was some sort of freak who could simultaneously gaze lovingly at my baby's adorable toes for hours while also desperately wishing I had a single hour to lose myself in a book. A nut-job who tearfully (my tears, the kid was fine) left my three-month-old son to return to work, while feeling nearly giddy with excitement to get back to my desk. But I kept it mostly to myself and a few select friends, because who else would understand? Little did I know how common these feelings were.

It wasn't until we (myself, husband, son, two cats and a dog) moved back to my home state of Maine in the beginning of 2015 that there was a noticeable shift. Due to my now longer work commute, and dislike of morning radio shows, I discovered the magic of podcasts. Thankfully, one of the very first podcasts I stumbled upon was *One Bad Mother,* hosted by Biz Ellis and Theresa Thorn. I was dumbfounded. Here were two mamas talking openly about things that SUCKED about motherhood. And here also was their podcast's official Facebook group, filled with *thousands* of mamas who also talked about such things. And who didn't judge. I was not a freak. And most notably—*I was not alone.* To say it was a game-changer would be an understatement. I felt understood, normal, emboldened ... and betrayed.

(continued on next page)

Why was this truth something I had to stumble upon? Why wasn't it public knowledge that early motherhood is *f-ing hard,* and sometimes dark, and that you will need help and you should have *zero* shame in asking for it? That you possibly will miss the person you were pre-motherhood, and that for some (if not most), it's vital to (re)discover yourself again, well before the kids go off to college? Once I realized how many other mamas felt the same as I did, I wanted more. I wanted to hear ALL the stories. But after searching around for an interview-format podcast where mamas mutually chatted about finding time for their own creativity and outlets amidst motherhood (and everything else), I came up short.**

So, what's an overwhelmed, sleep-deprived, artistically-stifled mama to do? Well, I *was* feeling like I needed a creative outlet, and thus, the **Who's Your Mama Podcast** was born! Nevermind that I had absolutely no idea *how* to actually make a podcast ... or that we were still "temporarily" living with my parents, with barely a room to ourselves, much less a "studio"—I had a PURPOSE! Luckily, I also had good friends available for encouragement, creative brainstorming and expertise in sound and recording, a small corner to occasionally prop up my home-made "sound booth," and a child who finally reliably slept (kind of). I started out interviewing my own inspirational mama friends, and from there the nominations *(and self-nominations!)* and connections grew. Not only had I found a new creative hobby, I was having fascinating, validating conversations, and adding to the larger (and ever-growing) narrative of what's acceptable for motherhood in today's society.

Sure, there were some hiccups along the way—mostly technical because, for better or worse, I didn't wait for "perfect" before plowing ahead—but creating the *Who's Your Mama Podcast* unlocked something in me that had been absent since I'd lost myself in motherhood. Not only my creativity, but a sense of community and connection to the bigger picture. And that then gave me the confidence to seek out opportunities to better connect to *local,* like-minded moms—like actively stepping up to join the board of a moms group that, up until that point, I had only been a halfhearted member. And that's when I decided I didn't want another new mama to *ever* feel the isolation that I had felt—and certainly not for as long as I did. I happened to have the graphic design tools *(hi there, expensive art school degree!).* Now it was time to create the toolkit.

**Times have changed/are changing! See the Resources section in the back.

Much in the same way that I tackled the podcast, I threw myself headlong into the creation of this very workbook, organization (and energy levels) be damned! And it was energizing ... *at first.* It wasn't long before I noticed that I was losing steam at an alarming rate. But why? I knew this project was in alignment with my passion and purpose, so why was I hitting a wall? After a number of weeks trying to power through, I finally surrendered to my lack of "productivity" and focused my attention inward once again. Little did I know at the time that this was a much-needed, and completely natural, phase of creation—the "Fertile Void." A gestational span of time (the length of which differs from person to person) where one intakes rather than outputs, all the while marinating in the creative juices simmering below the surface. It was during this phase that I participated in a local five-month women's circle ("On Being a Woman," led by Portland-based coach Lael Couper Jepson of SheChanges) and started really connecting with the writings and offerings of (also Portland-based) Kate Northrup, especially her online mamapreneur-focused "Origin Collective." And now, a full year later from when I confidently announced on my podcast and website that a workbook was "coming SOON," I am finally sitting down with a renewed sense of purpose to share my story, including the relatable—*and now blessedly long-past*—mama meltdown mentioned at the start of this introduction.

Thankfully, that aforementioned (figurative and literal) shit-show represents a scenario far less common in my life nowadays. I am now firmly in a place where I can easily ask for—and often simply *announce*—the time and space that I need to exist as an autonomous, creative, sane individual. And I don't apologize for any of it. This state of being didn't materialize overnight, and there are still speed bumps along the way, but hopefully my steps—often backward, sometimes forward, but ever onward—will allow me make your journey a little easier.

Before we get going, I want you to know that I *see* you, and I am holding space for you—within this workbook, and out in the world. Just remember that you are *entitled* to engage in activities that make you feel fulfilled, whole and inspired. You can, and *will,* figure this out, and the possibilities are end-less. And most importantly, you deserve this. Repeat: *You deserve this.* It's time to (re)discover the self-care you've been missing, creative or otherwise, and to say hello to yourself again—she missed you.

"I realized, and owned up to myself that I wasn't very happy. And over the next year, I started thinking about ways I could revisit myself as a person."

- Britney Gardner,
marketing photographer & brand strategist and host of
The Know, Like & Trust Show podcast
(*Who's Your Mama* · Season 1 · Episode 16)

D!SCLAIMER - DEDICAT!ON:

WARNING: This workbook content, while created for the purpose of inspiring and validating others, essentially comes from the creative (albeit, at times frazzled) mind of one individual—*me.* You may not agree with what is written. The words on these pages might make you so angry that you want to find me on the internet just to write some scathing review/comment/attack from behind the safe, anonymity of your computer. Please don't. I don't have time for it, and neither do you. If you do not/cannot relate to what is written here, *put the book down, back away, breathe deep.* Find something you can relate to. Move on. This book is not for you, *and that's ok.*

This book IS for...

...the mama who is so swayed by external opinions that she waits until the baby is asleep so that she can cry into the solitary dark of the nursery. Who can't seem to find the time to brush her hair, much less pursue a hobby she once deeply enjoyed—and who feels guilty about even *wanting* to have a hobby. Who cringes at the phrases "enjoy this season of motherhood!" or "they grow up so fast!" because right now she is in the trenches, the dark days, covered in poop and longing to feel like an autonomous human again. She tries to "embrace the season." She juggles all the balls. She puts on real pants, smiles at other moms out in the real world, and answers every well-meaning "How are you?" with "Great! Just greeeaaat!" Because that's what society *wants* to hear. But inside, she is wilting a little more each day.

...the mama who isn't so much discouraged by *outside* whispers, so much as the judgmental "committee" in her own head. Who knows full well that her creativity is a vital part of her life-force, and may even see others some-how "balancing" both motherhood and hobbies, yet is so in love with her children that she can't choose to "abandon" them for herself. And yet ... the pull is so strong that she can't simply sweep it under the rug. Her biggest obstacle is her deep-rooted, maternal instincts and her own torn heart.

(continued on next page)

...the mama who has started to realize that this societal cover-up is a load of crap. The mama who has started to hear the whispers—other mamas equally wistful about losing themselves after becoming moms, equally guilty that they feel this way, equally angry that they feel (or are told they should feel) guilty for wanting more. The mama who realizes she's not the only one. The mama who starts to ask for help, to make time for herself again—slowly, tentatively—until she realizes her kids are fine, she is fine (better, actually!) and the world has not imploded. She can do this. She *must* do this.

...the mama who is long past asking for time to herself, who instead simply states that she needs x at such time on such day and works out the help she needs with the other trusted, able-bodied humans in her life. Or, who firmly announces she needs a break when "momming-up" is pushing her toward the breaking point. Who has people in her life willing (or at the very least, *paid* to be willing) to take over when she's tapped out—or even better, who *offer* that help before she has to ask. Whose child/ren are even starting to understand that mama going out, or taking a break in a different area of the house, is just something that mama does, and that she still loves them and will be back, happily ready to jump back in—renewed and refreshed. Because this mama has realized the vital importance of time and space to rest, to regroup, to create. She has no interest in apologizing for it or in going back to how things were before she found this groove.

Now, I want to be crystal clear: I am in no way suggesting that we all must become EXACTLY who we were before kids. Whether we physically reproduce or not, we as humans have the *infinite* potential to continuously grow and change. And having children (biologically or not) transforms us in positive ways that are immeasurable. However, in response to anyone shaming you *against* finding your "pre-mama mojo" again: There is a strange, sabotaging insistence to staunchly tell mothers what they can and can't do after motherhood (including reclaiming themselves as individuals) that got us here in the first place—and the continuation of this narrow outlook just compounds the problem! I broke free and I now feel that it's my calling to encourage other mamas to (re)discover who they are as well.

Now, if you've read this far and still do not relate—again, *it's ok*. Please, continue to be your awesome version of a mama and I will continue to be mine. I promise, there's enough awesome mama-ness in the world for both of us. And, I'm actually glad you don't relate to my story. In fact, you should go tell *your* story, as I'm sure others will relate to YOU! We need more women sharing their stories—there is community, and great healing, to be found in such truth telling.

In fact, this workbook is dedicated to ALL the mamas—wherever you are in this journey, because I am right there with you, "individual card" firmly held aloft, in fist-pumping hand!

And please, keep in mind that my story, personal insights, and various calls to reflection, (re)discovery, and action may deeply resonate with you ... or they may not. Take what speaks to you and leave the rest (for now, or for a while—there is no timetable on this journey). And remember: *I am not telling you anything in these pages that you don't already know, deep in your bones.* So, trust—in your journey, and most importantly, dear mama, in yourself!

ONWARD!

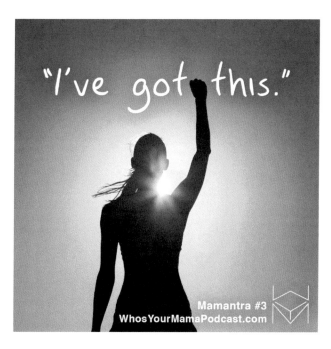

PART 1:
··· *Inward* ···

EXPECTATION

"The guilt doesn't really go away—
it becomes part of the motherhood
package. But there's so much we can
do ... to make it worth it. If you're gonna
feel guilty anyway, how are you going to
fill your time ... to really make it worth it?"

- Kathleen Ann Harper,
author and certified life (and crafting!) coach for moms
(*Who's Your Mama* · Season 1 · Episode 21)

•• (RE)DISCOVERY ••

It's #truth time, mamas. I know, I know ... you want to get to the *fun* stuff already! However, anyone who's stumbled into the self-help sector knows (however begrudgingly) that you have to find the root cause to your current challenge ... and bravely *lean in* to all the feels, instead of avoiding the experience. Only then can you find (often creative) solutions and begin to move on from there.

So, let's Unpack Expectations & (Re)Claim Creative Intentions:

How did you *think* life-after-motherhood (or becoming a mother) would be or would *feel* like?

_____

_____

_____

_____

_____

Where do you think these expectations came from? (Your upbringing, the media, a specific influence or moment in your life, etc.)

_____

_____

_____

_____

Which of these expectations were/are internal and/or external?

_____

_____

_____

_____

Describe the home environment/support system that you are currently surrounded with ... or not. How does this compare to what you were expecting at this stage in life?

Who do you want to be as a mother, wife, partner, sister, daughter, friend, etc.? *(Pick any or all of the above.)*

Who do you want to be as an *individual?*

What is the *creative* **life you want?**

Really take your time with these questions, and be as honest as you need to be. This is not the time to play nice or gloss over the facts. And if what you wrote ends up just bumming you out, never fear—we're going to rewrite that story next...

·· ACTION ··

Rewrite Your Story! Look over your answers to the (re)discovery above, and imagine now that you are the *heroine* of your story and every challenge you've experienced up until now is NOT a frustrating setback/failure, but an extremely interesting Season three plot twist that only adds to your dragon-slaying badassery. Feel free to adopt a Wonder Woman power stance as you hammer out the details, and don't hesitate to get really ambitious in how YOU decide your tale should end—*this is Hollywood material, mama!*

_____

_____

_____

_____

_____

_____

_____

_____

_____

_____

_____

__Go Deeper:__ If you want to get really woo-woo up in here, write your (re)discovery answers on a scrap of paper, then shred it, burn it, or release it on the wind/water. Recite any intention or invocation that feels right to you in the moment. Breathe deep.

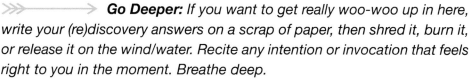

•• FURTHER READING ••

"Expectations are like dirty produce that's fresh from the farmer's market; they're hope covered in a layer of dirt that you'll want to wash away. Finding the hope underneath your expectations means coming clean and taking responsibility for your thoughts about what you think should happen."

- Kathleen Ann Harper, from *The Well-Crafted Mom:*
A Do-it-Yourself Guide to Making a Life You Love

INTUITION

"There is a specific ... artistic, creative energy that you want to save for your art. And if you use it elsewhere, you're kind of being emptied out."

- Shira Richter,
multidisciplinary visual artist and lecturer focused on the feminist politics of motherhood

(Who's Your Mama · Season 1 · Episode 18)

•• (RE)DISCOVERY ••

Yeah ... that last section was a tough one. Shake it off, take a deep, grounding breath and follow me:

You are walking along a quiet path in the woods, faint birdsong and sounds of a nearby stream can be heard. The season is late spring, thick moss covers the ground and peaceful old trees surround you on all sides. The sunlight is filtering down through the leaves, creating that perfect hue of fresh green all around. You are somehow both invigorated and calm, and ready to take on the day.

That was one of my "Happy Places." And I bet you have one (or more) as well. You know, the place you go to (either literally or figuratively) when you need to recharge. Your calm center, your Fortress of Solitude—whatever you call it, think of it like a reset button that activates your core/source of personal power.

Take a minute and go to your Happy Place (imagine that you're *really* there). *Got it?* **Now, write down or record as much of a description as you can:**

Look back on your Happy Place description and ask yourself the following:

Is it simply the *location* that relaxes you? Are sound, smell, and touch as important as what you're seeing? Does your Happy Place include a specific activity, action, or ritual? And most importantly—how do you *feel* while there? (*Repeat this exercise for however many Happy Places you have! Note any common themes.*)

Go Deeper: *Record a voice memo of yourself reading the description(s) of your Happy Place(s). Pop in some headphones and listen anytime you need to (literally) tune out.* **Bonus points for getting techy and layering some mystic music or birds chirping in the background!**

•• ACTION ••

Color Your Truth! For this exercise, you will need drawing paper, pencil & your coloring medium of choice (colored pencils, brush markers, crayons).

First, list some words or phrases that will instantly bring you to your Happy Place(s). Using my example, I could go with "peaceful green" or "sunlit path":

_____

_____

_____

Next, create a coloring page (either in the space opposite, or on a separate piece of paper) by decoratively writing the word or phrase that you decided on—feel free to bring back cursive or even bubble-letters! Then, surround the word(s) with geometric shapes, patterns, any design you choose. Think of the random doodles you used to make in the margins of your notebooks during school. Fill the page and then set it aside somewhere, out of the reach of tiny hands.

Now, the next time you feel like locking yourself in the bathroom, let your kids survive without your laser-focus and color away! Take a photo to share on social media with a fancy filter, or simply gaze at your masterpiece the next time you need some insta-calm.

•• FURTHER READING ••

"How much better is silence; the coffee cup, the table. How much better to sit by myself like the solitary sea-bird that opens its wings on the stake. Let me sit here for ever with bare things, this coffee cup, this knife, this fork, things in themselves, myself being myself."

- Virginia Woolf, from _The Waves_

RECLAMATION

"A personal identity ... was one thing I wanted to maintain—so if I painted every day ... even if they were in the room, I was still doing something that felt like it was me as an individual ... and I think that helped keep me sane."

- Delanie Holton-Fessler,
co-creator of The Craftsman & Apprentice
(*Who's Your Mama* · Season 1 · Episode 11)

•• (RE)DISCOVERY ••

I want you to connect with who you were—not just Before Children ("B.C."), but before this world stole some of the spark that lit your fire. Tap into your instinctual, unselfconscious, creative magic and encourage your inner child to emerge. She's gonna look different for everyone. And remember, there are no right or wrong answers ... just you being a good mother to yourself, to that still small voice, that fanner of the flames, that creative being that still lives inside of you!

Get yourself into a comfortable position, with as little surrounding noise and distraction as humanly possible, or put on some music if that helps you concentrate. Visualize yourself at a young age. *Take a few slow, deep breaths, and (Re)Connect With Your Inner Child:*

What were your favorite activities, creative hobbies, or outlets? What made you the happiest? The most relaxed? Feel the most free? Feel the most like your true self?

_____

_____

_____

_____

_____

What did you look forward to doing on the weekend? What did you like to do with your friends? What did you do when you were alone?

_____

_____

_____

_____

What were your favorite subject(s) in school? Did you enjoy learning new things? Being challenged? What skills do you remember proudly conquering at this time?

What did "creativity" mean to you at this age? Did you consider yourself "creative?" Was creativity encouraged at school and/or at home?

Who were you inspired by (famous or someone you knew in real life, a mentor perhaps)? What impact did they have?

What did you want to be when you grew up? What was your wildest, most secret dream?

_____

_____

_____

_____

_____

_____

_____

If you could travel back in time, what would you say to this younger version of yourself? And what words of wisdom could younger-you share with grown-up-you today?

_____

_____

_____

_____

_____

_____

_____

_____

_____

_____

_____

⟫⟫⟫————→ ***Go Deeper:*** *Repeat this exercise for the teen years, college, young adult, adult(ing) B.C., post-motherhood (including activities you enjoy doing with your kids).* ***Warning:*** *Once started, this list may never end or be complete ... but that's half the fun!*

•• ΛCTIǪN ••

Follow the Breadcrumbs! While communing with your inner child, did you (re)discover any creative outlet(s) that used to really light you up, or did any potential hobbies spring to mind—something that you've always wanted to try? Start poking around online, and create a vision board or two *(or three)* on Pinterest, to scroll through when you need an inspiration fix or a healthy reminder of your creative goals.

•• FURTHER READING ••

"Even though we have only heard or seen or dreamt a wondrous wild world that we belonged to once, even though we have not yet or only momentarily touched it, even though we do not identify ourselves as part of it, the memory of it is a beacon that guides us toward what we belong to, and for the rest of our lives."

- Dr. Clarissa Pinkola Estés, from *Women Who Run With the Wolves: Myths and Stories of the Wild Woman Archetype*

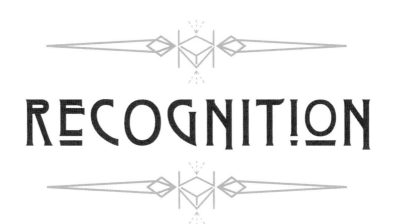

RECOGNITION

"Part of being 'well' mentally is recognizing yourself as a person first ... then as a mom, a wife, a sister. I'm taking care of ME so I can go home and be a better mom, wife, etc."

- Andrea Masters,
Assistant Director of Wellness at the University of Toledo
(*Who's Your Mama* · Season 1 · Episode 8)

·· (RE)DISCOVERY ··

Now that we've unpacked our expectations, found our "happy place" (or "places"), released our inner child, flexed our artistic muscles a bit, and most importantly, realized that wanting a creative (dare I say, *independent*) life is completely freakin' normal, let's get down to business.

WHO ARE YOU NOW? Time to play Strengths & Spin!

Describe yourself using only *positive* words. Include the gains and transformations you've made since becoming a mother (e.g. seamlessly multitasking, like a mother). HOT TIP: If you seem to only be coming up with negatives or weaknesses, play the game of "spin" and turn each into a positive or a strength (e.g. dramatic = passionate, pushover = nurturing) and reflect on how to use your newly spun powers only for good in the future *(for others AND for yourself)*:

If you're still struggling, ask a trusted friend, family member, your spouse, or your kids how they would lovingly describe you to others. I guarantee, you'll be touched and motivated by the words of your loved ones. Now, write it down before you brush it off:

Go Deeper: *Have fun with this exercise and turn it into a DIY TED Talk or "SuperSoul Session"*—Pretend you're live on stage and present your (well-deserved) awesomeness as a motivational speech. Or set a couple of expensive-looking wicker chairs out onto the lawn and have a close friend interview you while you both nod emphatically and fight back tears. Record for future posterity.*

*Disclaimer: *Neither I nor Who's Your Mama Media is associated with TED or SuperSoul Sessions/Oprah ... yet.*

·· ACTION ··

A Shrine* to Yourself! First, allow yourself to really soak in all your brilliance —the facets and edges alike. It's time to create a homage to YOU!

Find an empty cookie, mint or tea tin, gift box, or another unique box or container. Dig out those pieces of personal memorabilia you can't bear to throw out along with any scraps of miscellanea you've been saving for the sparks of inspiration they brought you (e.g. interesting matchbooks, postcards, beautiful wrapping paper, rocks or shells from your travels). Lastly, get out that stack of old magazines, some scissors and glue (I suggest a hot glue gun for mixed media).

Rip and cut and gather and rearrange, using only pieces that really speak to you. Play around with the layout before gluing everything into place but don't get too caught up in the momentous "permanence" of this shrine. Think of it as a visual representation of where you are _right now,_ at this moment in your life—an ever-changing individual on the threshold of (Re)Discovering Your Creativity.

 **_Go Deeper:_** _If you'd rather celebrate yourself in a completely different medium—go nuts! Or enlist a local artist (triple points for hiring a fellow mama!) to photograph or paint you in your glory, create a custom piece of jewelry or clothing, or even give you a tattoo to remind you of how amazing you are!_

·· FURTHER READING ··

"...I've learned one true thing about me. Maybe there is more to learn. _Hello soul, I am learning what you love. I will get more of this for us, I promise._ I have met my self and I am going to care for her fiercely. At least as fiercely as I care for everyone else in my life. I will not abandon, ignore, or lose myself again."

- Glennon Doyle, _Love Warrior_

I prefer using the traditional nicho or shadowbox style for my "shrines" (be sure to first check out the work of Kathy Cano-Murillo — the "Crafty Chica" — and even poke around on Pinterest a bit for inspiration), but feel free to skip the container and simply create a 2D collage, on a piece of cardstock or in the space below:

INTERMISSION

AFFIRMATION

"It's about making sure, as moms, that we don't put unwarranted, unnecessary pressure or guilt on ourselves as we're figuring it out, because everyone's going to go through that emotional turmoil ... finding their groove."

- Lauren Bercovitch,
filmmaker, producer, director & blogger at Grown Up Party
(Who's Your Mama · Season 1 · Episode 10)

·· (RE)DISCOVERY ··

Ok, right now you know you're an entire bucket of awesome-sauce, but what about a week from now *(heck, tomorrow)* when the shiz hits the fan and you suddenly think you're the worst mother/wife/partner/friend/person/sunbutter-sandwich-maker ever? You're gonna want to have some fist-bumping affirmations at the ready, to remind you that you are amazing, and *entitled* to be a creative individual.

Wisdom & Affirmations: Think of some of your favorite quotes or pieces of advice (well-known or that fabulous phrase your Nana used to say). *You know, the ones that remind you to keep your head up high, to listen to your heart, to dance and sing like nobody's watching...*

Also, think about the great advice *you* give to others when they come to you with their troubles (*you are a wise woman, too!*). Write 'em down:

•• ACTION ••

Make-Your-Own Mamantra®! I have always loved inspirational quotes (especially good-looking ones on Pinterest) so, graphic designer that I am, I started writing and designing some specifically for mamas ... and BOOM: *Mamantras® were born!*

And, now it's *your* turn: Start with your favorite quotes or pieces of advice from the (Re)Discovery—condense into sound bites if necessary—and use Canva (or Photoshop, if you prefer) to make a Pinterest-style inspirational quote out of it. **HOT TIP:** Unsplash.com has gorgeous and free photos that you can use as backgrounds *(see: the photos in this very workbook!)* and DaFont.com has hundreds of nicely-designed, free fonts. Once your Mamantra® is complete, share profusely on social media and save as your home screen. And, be sure to credit your source (especially if it's YOU!).

⫸—————➤ *Go Deeper: As with the description of your happy place(s), record voice memos of yourself reciting your inspirational Mamantras®— extra points if you can layer some meditation music in the background! Pop in the headphones and listen anytime you need to (literally) tune out.*

•• FURTHER READING ••

"I recognize that the word *entitlement* has dreadfully negative connotations, but I'd like to appropriate it here and put it to good use, because you will never be able to create anything interesting out of your life if you don't believe that you're entitled to at least try. Creative entitlement doesn't mean behaving like a princess, or acting as though the world owes you anything whatsoever. No, creative entitlement simply means believing that *you are allowed to be here,* and that—merely by being here—you are allowed to have a voice and a vision of your own."

— Elizabeth Gilbert, *Big Magic*

PART 2:
··· *Outward* ···

PREPARATION

"Don't get discouraged! Sometimes it just takes a little time to figure out what you want to do and how to manifest that passion ... when the time is right, and you set your intentions to it, things really blossom."

- Kristen Taylor,
author, co-creator of Live Yum & newly certified meditation
instructor and founder of Wellspring Meditation
(Who's Your Mama · Season 1 · Episode 1)

•• ACTION ••

Prep Your List! This one's a quickie meant to get the wheels in motion. Refer back to your list of possible creative outlets from the "Follow the Breadcrumbs" exercise. Narrow it down to your top three, or even a top choice if one is particularly lighting you up. See if there's a how-to book at the library or bookstore, a video or course online, or a local class. And ask around—you may already know someone in your circle or community who has the talent you're hoping to (re)learn!

Make an organized list of resources, costs, and schedules to return to when ready:

•• FURTHER READING ••

"Passion will always move you in the direction of your authentic self...And by the way, passion doesn't need to be constantly fiery and all consuming; it can be a steady curiosity and commitment...Genuine curiosity and sincere interest are burning coals that can warm you for a good, long time. Your curiosity is your growth point. Always."

- Danielle LaPorte, *The Fire Starter Sessions: A Soulful + Practical Guide to Creating Success on Your Own Terms*

COLLABORATION

"The place I've snapped into is one of defiance. I'm really mercenary ... I'm simply going to push back on any expectations that I do things that take me away from my most important priorities."

- Kelly Diels,
author/blogger & creator of the Feminist Marketing School
(*Who's Your Mama* · Season 1 · Episode 12)

•• ACTION ••

Slow Down, Support, Outsource. It's all well and good to know *what* you want, but figuring out *how* to make it actually happen is an important piece of this puzzle. So, let's talk logistics. While creating this workbook, I sent out a survey to fellow mamas in hopes of discovering common threads to obstacles (internal or external) that we all face while attempting to maintain a creative practice. Two almost universal answers were **Time** and **Support.**

Ye olde adage is true: "It takes a village." But sometimes that village is made up of unexpected parts. Regardless of how the support comes in, allowing yourself to accept this help and free up your time for creative pursuits is a powerful form of self-care. A buzz word to be sure, but regular self-care is vital to your health, happiness, sanity, and yes, to your creativity—*and not at all selfish!*

Try one (or all) of these ideas on for size:

• **List your go-to relax/recharge activities.** This could be a creative outlet or just something that always improves your mood (glass-of-wine-in-the-bath-with-door-locked totally counts!). When you desperately need a break, pick something from the list. Better yet, pick something from the list and do it *before you get to the point of needing a break.* Even if you feel like you "don't have the time" anymore. Do it, even if you have to cut something else out (Facebook scrolling, anyone?). Future-self will thank you!

• **Disconnect to reconnect.** Unsubscribe/unplug from email lists, social media, and any mindless activity that makes you feel drained instead of fired up. If necessary, plug your phone into the wall, away from your body, if the temptation to zone out is too strong. Utilize the reminder or alert feature on your phone, if only to take a mental load off for the little things.

- **Rally the support you need!** You'll be surprised how many people in your life will be more than happy to help if you just ASK. You do not have to do it all yourself. And, *it's actually generous of you to allow others the joy of helping.* Be specific in your ask, and accept the help once it's offered.

- **The village is wide.** If you still need more support, do *not* feel guilty sending your kid to daycare (even part-time) or hiring a babysitter. At the very least, enjoy a delicious coffee and an interesting short-read on your phone while your child(ren) goes hog-wild at the safely-padded trampoline park. *Remember to breathe.*

- **Outsource it!** What time-consuming tasks can you hand off? Cleaners can be hired to come to your house once or twice a month—just often enough to take the weight of the dust-covered world off your shoulders. If money is tight, see if you can barter for professional services. Or learn to accept that the vacuuming doesn't get done as often or as meticulously as you might prefer. Everyone will live, *especially you!*

•• FURTHER READING ••

"…I also see 'no' as a place and a space, and not necessarily an act. No's are the entrances to my burrows as a rabbit. They allow me to go underground from time to time, so I can make the most of my yes's…I no longer surround it by explanation or chase it with an apology. I also don't ask for permission or expect that others will understand. I simply head into my burrow, leaving others to make of it what they will."

- Lael Couper Jepson, *Unscripted: A Woman's Living Prayer*

"You cannot come to know the depths of the purpose of your life, however, if you are not willing to release those parts of your life that are no longer necessary."

- Caroline Myss, *Sacred Contracts: Awakening Your Divine Potential*

ACTIVATION

"Everything just grows to fill the space that you have ... Being a parent now, I have to be more decisive. And it's awesome—it's a really good practice to trust your instincts."

- Molly O'Rourke,
owner of floral & event design studio One & Supp
(Who's Your Mama · Season 1 · Episode 17)

·· ACTION ··

Make a Plan, Light the Match. You've come a long way, mama! You've faced your expectation-demons, dusted off that "individual card" that had somehow ended up at the bottom of the drawer, invoked the creative flame that still burns within, and been generous enough (with yourself and others) to rally the support you need/deserve.

Remember, you have very consciously been working up to this point—your ducks are in a row and you are *entitled* to pursue what lights you up.

Now, it's go-time:

• **Simplify your goal(s)** into a sentence or two. Knowing exactly (or even partially) what you want to accomplish—and how you want to *feel*—will help you keep your "eye on the prize" when the going gets tough.

• **Start small.** Revisit your nicely organized list of research and resources from the Preparation section. Pick what seems most doable to start (also known as "low-hanging fruit") then list the sequence of action steps that will get you where you want to be. Work backward, if that helps. Rally that uber-organized friend to objectively help break down your to-dos into manageable bites, while still remaining aligned with your end goal(s).

• **Schedule the support** you will need for the dates and times you'll be working toward your goal(s). Again, do not be afraid to ask, do not feel guilty for outsourcing, and graciously accept the help you are given.

• **Choose your planner of choice.** It can be digital or paper, high tech and fancy or super basic. The most important thing is to work with how *you* best organize/plan/create. Take those times you asked for and scheduled help and enter them in your planner as "otherwise engaged."

• **Add due dates *(but only if that doesn't cause added anxiety)*.** Or, go "back to school" and create a curriculum out of your goal and modules out of your action steps to achieve at your own pace.

- **Stay in motion and stick with it.** Join a group (locally or online) or enlist an equally motivated friend as an accountability partner for weekly/monthly check-ins. Start a blog or report on your progress in status updates. Make a plan for continuous engagement with your creative practice and keep up the momentum in a positive way.

- **Have fun with it!** Plan a gallery opening, a reading, a recital, a dinner party, or any relevant debut surrounding your crowning achievement (or latest stepping stone accomplishment). Design the invites and wear that dress you never get to wear anymore. Whether you celebrate with only your spouse, kids, close family, all of your friends, or the whole town, go as big or as intimate as you want to go!

- **Invite other mamas to (re)discover their creativity too!** Obviously, point them in the direction of this Workbook (and the *Who's Your Mama Podcast*), but please, ***share your story as well.*** Your decision to make time for what lights you up will most certainly inspire them to do the same!

- Remember to **CELEBRATE THE SMALLEST OF VICTORIES** as you make creativity an important part of your life again. *You've got this!*

•• FURTHER READING ••

"When we have a shift like this, it's as though a flash flood has washed the path behind us away. If we turn back the way we've come, there are no tracks, no clear way to go, and no trace of the old way. So our only choice becomes the choice of moving forward."

- Kate Northrup, *Money: A Love Story*

"My future seemed to stretch out before me like a straight road... Now there is a bend in it. I don't know what lies around the bend, but I'm going to believe that the best does."

- L.M. Montgomery, *Anne of Green Gables*

RESOURCES (AKA: SHINE THEORY*)

FURTHER READING:

(mentioned within and worth mentioning)

• *The Well-Crafted Mom: A Do-it-Yourself Guide to Making a Life You Love* by Kathleen Ann Harper

• *The Waves* by Virginia Woolf

• *Women Who Run With the Wolves: Myths and Stories of the Wild Woman Archetype* by Dr. Clarissa Pinkola Estés

• *Love Warrior* by Glennon Doyle

• *Big Magic* by Elizabeth Gilbert

• *The Firestarter Sessions: A Soulful + Practical Guide to Creating Success on Your Own Terms* by Danielle LaPorte (+ everything she writes/says)

• *Unscripted: A Woman's Living Prayer* by Lael Couper Jepson

• *Sacred Contracts: Awakening Your Divine Potential* by Caroline Myss

• *Money: A Love Story* by Kate Northrup

• *Anne of Green Gables* by L.M. Montgomery

• *The Artist's Way: A Spiritual Path to Higher Creativity* by Julia Cameron

• *Rising Strong: How the Ability to Reset Transforms the Way We Live, Love, Parent, and Lead* by Brené Brown

• *Untame Yourself: Reconnect to the Lost Art, Power and Freedom of Being a Woman* by Elizabeth DiAlto

• *In the Company of Women* by Grace Bonney

• *Playing Big: Practical Wisdom for Women Who Want to Speak Up, Create, and Lead* by Tara Sophia Mohr (& her "Expect to Be a Revolutionary" post)

• *The Alchemist* by Paulo Coelho

*Google "Shine Theory" by Ann Friedman

PODCASTS:

- *One Bad Mother* with Biz Ellis and Theresa Thorn

- *Untangled* with Alana Helbig

- *Raising Women* with Johanna Rossi

- *Happier* with Gretchen Rubin and Elizabeth Craft

- *In Her Voice* with Kelly Covert

- *The Crafty Chica Show!* with Kathy Cano-Murillo

- *Mother's Quest* with Julie Neale

- *The Boss Mom Podcast* with Dana Malstaff

- *She Explores* with Gale Straub

- *The Kate & Mike Show* with Kate Northrup and Mike Watts

- *The Recapture Self Podcast* with Beryl Ayn Young

- *RoamHowl* with Jennifer Gardner

- *Magic Lessons* with Elizabeth Gilbert *(on hiatus)*

- *Side Hustle School* with Chris Guillebeau

- *The Accidental Creative* with Todd Henry

GROUPS/PROGRAMS:

- SheChanges coaching *(Portland, ME & beyond)*, "On Being a Woman" 5-month Circle *(Portland, ME)*, and "In Her Words" 6-Week Writing Series *(anywhere)* with Lael Couper Jepson **SheChanges.com**

- The Desire Map Guide + Planner, and The Firestarter Sessions private Facebook group w/ Danielle LaPorte **DanielleLaPorte.com**

- Origin Collective: Reimagining Entrepreneurship and Motherhood Together with Kate Northrup **OriginCollective.com**

- The Mother's Quest one-on-one coaching, virtual circle, and private Facebook group with Julie Neale **MothersQuest.com**

- The Well-Crafted Mom: Life-Changing Coaching + Crafts for Moms, mini-retreats, and private Facebook group with Kathleen Ann Harper **TheWellCraftedMom.com**

- An Artist in Residency in Mother-hood with Lenka Clayton *(free)* **artistresidencyinmotherhood.com**

- Boss Moms, One Bad Mother & similar Facebook groups *(free)*

GRATITUDE

So many voices—especially women's voices—have lifted and inspired me to follow my *own* intuition and listen to my *own* voice with deeper trust.

I am lucky to have many cheerleaders in my inner circle to thank: My own mother, Lesli (and *her* mother, my Nana Bernice), for showing me that you're never too young (or too old) to make creativity a top priority. My mother-in-law, Tracey, for truly exemplifying that "the village" still exists and is more than happy to help. My old-schooler Angela, for being the first to hear (and to humor) my idea for bringing *Who's Your Mama* into this world. My rock(star) Sarah who—despite being too busy with three boys and a community to clothe to even have the time to understand what a podcast *was*—still unwaveringly supported whatever crazy project I was up to (and whatever crazy feels I was feeling). My soul sister Shannon, for continuously reminding me of the *why* of what I was doing (and for giving me a "deadline" so I could finally get out of my own way). Coven-leader Lael, for shining a light at the crossroads so that I could see the breadcrumbs more clearly. All the family and friends who have sent encouragement along the way, especially while I was half-buried in the deep soil of the Fertile Void. My 22 *(and counting!)* podcast guests, including those early ones—the "in real life" friends who enthusiastically agreed to jump on board. And guest #21—Kathleen—for graciously coming through on a (very) long-ago offer to professionally proofread this little workbook. We are the revolutionaries.

And let's not forget the men: My dad, Neal, for always encouraging the rebel in me. My Papa George, for rightfully considering himself a "writer," even without ever being published. Charlie, for the technical know-how. And my boys—my husband Butch and son James—for showing such support, not only for this project, but for my inherent, *entitled* human need for ongoing, restorative creative space. You are part of the solution.

CRED!TS

PODCAST GUESTS *(in order of appearance)*:

Kristen Taylor & Liz Price-Kellogg, Dr. Tamara Avant, Stacy Zarin Goldberg, Grey Catsidhe, Savannah Patraw, Dr. Jocelyn Mitchell, Bev Feldman, Andrea Masters, Kate Fisher, Lauren Bercovitch, Delanie Holton-Fessler, Kelly Diels, Sarah Cottrell, Rhea Pechter, Amber Hobbins, Britney Gardner, Molly O'Rourke, Shira Richter, Kelly Covert, Lisa Porter, Kathleen Ann Harper, Lesli Weiner.

WORKBOOK DESIGN AND LAYOUT:

Me! I'm a graphic designer by day *(and a fierce fighter for the creative rights of mamas by night)*. See my work and contact me to collaborate at: **DivineConception.net**

PHOTOS:

Author photo by Noelle Libby of no frills farm.

Front cover: Nadi Whatisdelirium. Back cover: Gaelle Marcel. Interior photos: Christopher Sardegna, Sunny Au8ust, Joshua Ness, Samuel Zeller, Rifqi Ali Ridho, Andrew Tanglao, Julie Johnson, Liam Simpson, Charlz Gutiérrez De Piñeres, Ryan Moreno *(via Unsplash.com)*.

TYPEFACES:

Display font: Dyer Arts and Crafts, by Typo-Graf *(via Dafont.com)*

Body font: Helvetica Neue

All content within/online © Who's Your Mama Media/Corinne Mockler

WANT MORE WHO'S YOUR MAMA?

Corinne Mockler
Creator/Producer/Host/Author
at Who's Your Mama Media
WhosYourMamaMedia.com

The (Re)Discovering Creativity After Motherhood Workbook, (re)fillable PDF and Video Lessons is the framework for maintaining a creative identity while raising a family that I created based on my own personal journey of rediscovery. A (re)fillable PDF version and Video Lessons are available for purchase directly from my website.

The **(Re)Discovering Creativity After Motherhood Workshop Series** is for mothers ready to take the first step toward pursuing personal fulfillment through creative hobbies, outlets, and activities. The group atmosphere provides validation and accountability as we discuss and move through the Workbook framework together. These workshops are ongoing.

The ***Stay Creative* Facebook Group** provides accountability, support, and inspiration for creative mamas who have already purchased the Workbook and/or attended a Workshop and want to take a deeper dive.

The ***Who's Your Mama Podcast*** features chats with inspiring women who are balancing motherhood while still pursuing the things they love, both personally and professionally. Be sure to subscribe for new episodes!

VISIT WhosYourMamaMedia.com for these offerings...*and more!*

FOLLOW Who's Your Mama on Facebook, Instagram, and Pinterest

All content within/online © Who's Your Mama Media/Corinne Mockler

(RE)DISCOVERY
••• *Continued* •••

Corinne Mockler // Who's Your Mama Media

Follow the breadcrumbs...

Made in the USA
Monee, IL
10 March 2022

92642600R00043